Beauty

BEAUTY

By
Marquita Graham

PUBLISHED by PARABLES
Earthly Stories with a Heavenly Meaning

Beauty
Marquita Graham

Published By Parables
February, 2019

All Rights Reserved. No part of this book may be reproduced or utilized in any form or by any means, electronic or mechanical, including photocopying, recording, or by any information storage and retrieval system, without permission in writing from the author.

ISBN 978-1-945698-63-7
Printed in the United States of America

Readers should be aware that Internet Web sites offered as citations and/or sources for further information may have been changed or disappeared between the time this was written and the time it is read.

I don't blame them

They're doing as expected

Now it's your turn

Warning ! !

The contents you are about to read have a little kick to them, if you know what I mean.

My life story is one of many that gives you a clear view into the mind of a true black woman.

Don't you know! A woman who has suffered the parables of gangsta life ,and a house ,wife in the same life time. Hopefully giving inspiration to young girls around the world, in such a way that compels them to do better and make grand decision in their lives. I am no saint by far, but I am a beacon of hope. Someone who can tell you what it feels like to live a double life, and still feel slightly unsatisfied. As you read my story just ask yourself this one question for me. Who am I?

Beauty who I am? Said the mirror looking back at me Clearly not the one I use to be .So I ask you again who am I ? A child of my mother and father… this I know . A flower planted by faith Afraid to truly grow. Afraid to let others know who I truly am? So just like you, and you, and you I stuff myself down in a tiny box of thoughts buried deep down in a heart of true forgiving others for turning red in my presence all the while I find myself turning blue.Than a different hue in god's view .Not me I say one day. I will not lay around and play with my life with my kind of love no!, not at all. Today I will stand up… and become tall. Show the world Marquita has a purpose Marquita will not die. Marquita is real to the bone, and the realest thing I can ask myself is who am I?

INTRODUCING

On September 17, 1983 in San Francisco, CA a star was born into the arms of Charlotte and Troy Harrington. Who both probably sat emotionless, in a state of shock, truly amazed at the sight of their new beloved daughter" me"... Marquita Harrington. An army hospital by the name of Letterman's was the scene for my coming out party (do not get clever in your thoughts critics and haters alike), but you get the picture. At times I wonder what my parents actually felt staring down at my tiny little face, afraid they might break me, or something. You know how everyone holds a new baby with that scared feelings! Anyway there I was, a love child, conceived with great admiration and thought. Ohhh ! How sweet is that ?

Quick history lesson: I was born on my great grandmother's day of birth. Mrs. Grace Thelma Harrington, a beautiful angel beyond words. Born 1907 " the golden age " where rights for black people had no place in this country. (A lot has changed as you see!)

Forgive me for my sarcasm but a realist I am to the heart. December 6th 1865, only 42 years earlier, and my great grandma would have been a slave. That is crazy to think, but not crazy to comprehend you know! I am just truly thankful for all her sacrifices that she made in her life to see the brightness of future times and generations that followed her. I always said "I have my grandmother's power, and my father's heart… which is saying a lot if you know my family.

TABLE OF CONTENTS

Chapter One : Beauty

Chapter Two : This Little Light of Mind

Chapter Three: Complications

Chapter Four : Deal with Your drama or not !

Chapter Five: Moving to fast

Chapter Six : Could It Be Love

Chapter Seven : Dead End Road

Chapter eight : Hope Finds A Home

Chapter Nine : Just When You Think You Have Seen It All

Chapter Ten : Thank You God ... for real !

Chapter 11 : The Future Has A Face of Beauty

Chapter 12 : Go Hard or Go To Hell

Chapter One

When I was one years old, my legs was burned with an iron. My mom told me that I climbed up on chair, than on a table where the iron sat burning red hot. Apparently I was playing with the iron, and got third degree burn from my thigh to my knee. Due to the severity of the burn I had to be airlifted to another hospital in California. Crazy huh ! What is even more crazy is how years later there is no scar in the space where the burn mark use to be. I covered it up with a tattoo that says (I taste like candy) do not hate ! Anyway I told you that little story to add . I believe beauty is not what happens to us, but how we feel about ourselves after it happens. No one can take away from you, nothing , you do not give them. Remember the scars do not define us ... they remind us... we are beautiful no matter what. Growing up I lived a very spoiled childhood. My dad gave us a taste of the good life beyond the normal. I am the oldest, and the only girl, so when I say i had the run of the mill it is a bold statement. I remember being scared out of my mind on the airplane flying to Germany. My dad got stationed out there for a furnishing part of his army career. My baby brother, Everett Michael Harrington, was born out there, Black German. As I recall it rained a lot over there, oddly bringing the snails out instead of the worms. I use to dance in the rain like a white kid. (Laugh if you want to, but you guys know black kids do not be playing in the rain !) I did though, and I enjoyed free and appreciated. I reached getting twenty dollars for every week a, on my report card. In grade school my family, and I lived on this army base, so every two weeks my father would spend $200-$500 at the commissary, and at the PX. Which was good eating for all you doubters. Who do not know what that is, just ask someone ... they will tell you how true it is. From the sixth grade to the 9th grade I played basketball for my middle school. I was the point guard on every team I ever played for. I also ran track, and field in seventh grade until my junior year. School for me was pretty easy, seeing how I was smart and one of the cool kids. I had great grades, and dressed nice everyday. I really enjoyed running Cross County in high school, and the dance team. Here is a crazy though, by the tenth grade we were back in the states, living in Colorado. I remember Columbine High School that year. My dance team went to cheerleading championship, and placed

2nd a month before those two kids shot up their school. I attended a school called William J. Palmer that year. I had a grand time , and grew a lot from those years in school. To all the kids in school today, if you do not mind me saying please get as much education as you can, because trust me when I say it will be your bread, and butter later in life.

Beauty the idea of beauty in our modern day society is getting an overdue makeover.

We are starting to see with true eyes, how beauty has many faces to call home, and giving truth to our future generations to come. Most kids nowadays take body shaming to another level- committing suicide to combat not feeling beautiful enough. Walking around halls feeling unaccepted by their peers and the world. The moment we call ourselves putting a standard on something as complex as beauty, is a grave down fall in our society.Beauty is a rare entity. Something we must keep a watchful eye on in order to have a grand perspective. Standards are set at a certain level, forcing us to jump through hoops to meet such a quota. But what happens when we do not measure up to a standard that seems to be forever changing ? As a young girl, full of ambition, and vigor, I never really noticed how much pressure people put on young girls.Forcing them to evaluate themselves ,or place themselves in superficial categories (the pretty girls, the weird girl's etc. etc. etc

This cycle continues, with each title adding another level of pressure to the complex element that is true beauty. Like seriously , who defines beauty in our society? The magazines we worship, and snatch off the shelves? The same magazines that tell us not to be normal, and relax in our own comfortable skins. Here's a funny fact: think about all the beautiful artifacts we have in our world. All the landscapes that demand a state of awe.(The Hoover Dam,Tag Mahan, Angkor watt, Golden Gate Bridge, Eiffel Tower, and International Space station are all different in their own way, but beautiful. Nonetheless, we as humans, try our best to destroy them, or steal away their essence. As we come to an end of my childhood chapter .I express something that took me to a long time to get over. When my mother was seven months pregnant with me she broke her hip getting out of the bathtub. Therefore she sent my older sister, Charnicka Williams, to Gary, Indiana under the custody of my aunt Darlene Gray. At the time my father was in the army, and did not trust anyone in California to babysit my sister. My mother had to stay in the hospital until I was born. My aunt Darlene was living with her first husband, James Gray, and his younger brothers. She worked a lot of hours at Wendy's so she would have her husband little brothers baby sit my sister, my cousin Tiffany, and my cousin Jamie. My aunt's husband was busy smoking crack cocaine, and chasing women, so my sister's dad asked my aunt's brother-in laws if he could pay them to bring my sister to the corner store. Eight hours later they told my aunt Darlene someone had kidnapped my older sister. But truthfully my sister's father took her to the courthouse, and told them that my mother was in California (painting her in a bad light) as if she abandoned her. Sneaky, Sneaky. My aunt, and her in laws were never truthful with my mother. She had idea of this meticulous scheme to win custody of her child, and paint her as a misfit mother. In addition, my mother's older brother (Charles Turner) was a Gary, Indiana police officer at the time. Now put yourself in my mother's shoes, and ask yourself how would you feel if you were in the hospital with a broken hip, pregnant, and completely confused about the whereabouts of your first born child. Than the people who you supposedly trust tell you that your child has been kidnapped only to find out a plot of deception was taking place. That is a hard pill to swallow. My mother went back , and forth to Gary, Indiana trying to clear her name, and win back custody of my sister. Since he was a toddler, and not potty trained yet, my younger brother, Everett Harrington, went with my mother. Eventually my mother got split custody of my sister with her baby's father. But my father ,being a true family man, sent for basically the whole family to come and live in Colorado Springs, CO. I can not say what he felt at that time, but from my observation it seemed like he wanted to make my mother happy by bringing her sister , and entire family to Colorado Springs. He also brought his side of the family together, being his brother, his mother, and his father out to Colorado. Sadly though that was a very rough year for my family. We lost my great grandmother, Grace Thelma Harrington, and my Uncle James Gray died from cancer five months later. Those deaths taught me a valuable lessons that I currently live by til this day. Cherish your loved ones while they are alive. People are not perfect but the will to love them through all the pain, and hurt gives you purpose to say "I Love you". My freshman year of high school, I worked at Wendy's with my best friend Danielle. A part time job while we were in school. It was cool for us to get a sense of being independant , and learning how the real world works. The summer of my tenth grade year,I worked at the Evergreen Cemetery, as a clerk assistant. A cemetery you say! Yes, and it was my first full time job. Forty hours a week. I brought my own school clothes, and school shoes. I got my nails did every chance I could. I brought myself fancy jewelry, and i had money in my pocket book to spend. It went straight to my head , I must say. Simply because I ran away at the age of fifthteen years old. Living with the OG 81 Crips took me in, seeing how I was dating one of their family members at the time. His name being Patric Anton Rucker Jr. I also lived with my best friend Natalie Arrington, and her aunt who was twenty five years old. She was an old hoe to be honest, but who am I to judge nowadays. Anyway Natalie's aunt knew all the older gangstas , and army men on Fort Carson army base. I sold drugs, and liquor to stay a float. Started smoking cigarettes, and weed like a Jamaican. I got pregnant with my oldest daughter Imani Rucker at the age of fifthhteen years old. I started maintain my lifestyle everyday. New outfits , and a nice shoes game had me in the mall every chance I got. After I got exhausted with living with Natalie, and her aunt. I had Patric come from Baltimore Maryland, and get us a house together. It was the two of us, and his three friends paying the rent together. :Patric's friend had a father in jail, and needed us to stay there, and house sit until he got out of prison.

I also was taking GED classes at the same time. I married at the age of sixteen years old to Patric Anton Rucker, a month after our daughter was born. The date was March 16,2001. I had my own apartment by now at the Carlton Manor Apartments. A one bedroom that my mother co signed for at the time. Patric's credit was so bad at the time, due to his parents destroying his credit as a child. :Putting things in his name. Wise words to the young girls out there in the world "Remember there is nothing wrong with waiting to grow up. Give yourself the paper time to enjoy your early childhood please. Sometimes we move too fast in life , unaware of how faster life moves ahead of us. Just love yourself enough to listen to what I'm saying…. You are beautiful remember." When you are in love there is nothing you wouldn't do for them , they stay in your mind. Everytime you think of them a smile appears across your face you are blind. You only want to make them happy at times you might not eat. Might say things that make you cry. You just don't want to make a mistake. You don't want to make a mistake. You don't want to hurt them, you don't lie to them. You are on your best, when you are in love your soul connects to them, you feel them even when they're not around you. You try to understand their past troubles, when they are happy...you are happy. When they are sad ../.you are sad as well. You smell them while they sleep, You just know. No one has to tell you when you're in love , you just know, and than if you're lucky. If you lucky ... You grow.

What Do We Want

We must all remember that it is very important to know what we want out of life.

Some of us feel we know what we want, but find ourselves confused at certain times of our lives. I believe it is best to be very clear about the direction of your life path . You can get off the path, and find yourself lost in your own fallacy. Do me a favor: ask yourself right now what direction is my life headed toward? In a year's time where do I want to be in life? How is my relationship now? What are my do's, and my don'ts?

How much money would I like to be making , or earning ? These things are only a few of things in life that should be running through your mind as you grow more into adulthood.

A closed mouth doesn't get fed.

Chapter Two

This little light of Mind

This little light of mine, I'm going to let it shine … this little light of mine, I'm going to let it shine … this little light of mine, I'm going to let it shine … let shine, let it shine, let it shine" I heard some of you guys singing along, as that song is probably one of the most known songs in the world. For good reasons as well. If you listen closely to the lyrics of that song, you will hear how impactful it can be on someone's life. I believe we are all similar to light bulbs. Having a certain type of shine to us many people take for granted . Some bulbs are brighter than others, and some bulbs burn out quicker than others as well. Take some our greatest music artist of all time, some were taken to soon while others ended their lives before their time. I always felt as if my mind was a little different than others. I knew this throughout my childhood, but as the story goes on you will see how we tend to forgot how bright our light truly has the power to be. "Remember who you are before someone tells you who you should be". The only thing I remember was my daughter called my dad , and my brother Everett. Who came through the door of our apartment so fast that i was where the hell did they come from? Anyway my father jumped on Patric in a crazy rage which shocked me to see my father in that light.Out of nowhere my mother saying screaming " in the blood of jesus!"That's the only thing that made my dad stop beating him down.It was crazy scene I must say. But my dad told me to get my things and get in the car with our daughter.I did my things, and get in the car with our daughter.I did but you guys know how it is when you're in love with someone. I'm the typing of woman who believe in his good side, which is not a good example for my daughters, and sons at the time . I had to learn to love myself in order to be able to love someone else." Never let anyone abuse you , or use you, and do not feel guilty about your situation." You know when you're in love because there is nothing you won't do for that person. They stay on your mind. You don't want to make a mistake. You only want to make them happy. Sometimes you might not eat, or sleep over them. You always want to be on your best.There is an odd soul connection between the two of you.You defend them against all odds. When their hurting, it hurts you as well. As I took my vows, just like many others, I wanted to believe

Beauty

in what me in Patrick had. We were the greatest front marriage known to mankind. I remember the time I tasted my own blood. Patric, and I were talking smack to one another, and trust me it got terrrr 2. At one point in time in our marriage all we did was fight. He said something to me , and I shot some quick remark back at him. You know the kind of remark that gets under your skin that's what I hit him with. Well I guess he could not take , and punched me dead in my face. Right to the lips his fist went. Big mistake. I fought him back like Tina Turner. He hit me again , and pushed me hard as he could. I fell to the ground the impact. I had to put a protection order against Patric for the following reasons? I was twenty two years old at the time. Patric climbed through my apartment window, which at the time was a bottom floor apartment at 907 East Santa Fe street. Most people call it by its formal name-Payne Chapel Housing over there by Hillside. But anyway, Patrick took the screen off my daughter's window, and had my daughter Imani in his arms already when I came to check on her. I was like what the hell !He was calling for our other daughter lovely to jump in his arms as well. I ran out of the building as fast as I could, but Patrick took off running like a track star with our daughter in his arms. By the time I reached the parking lot, the car speeded away with Patric, and my daughter gone. m y heart broke into a million pieces at that moment. He had planned the whole thing quite querulously if you ask me, but that stuff work. He had been stalking the apartment for a few weeks to pull off a move like that. I got calls from him, threatening to not bring our daughter back to me. Saying things like he was going to keep her away from me forever. My dad told me not to call the police on Patric , because he said Imani was his daughter as well , and no harm would come to her in his care. After a week of all that nonsense I called the Police, and was told I had to put a protection order against him. I mean we were Husband , and wife, so he had rights to the rights to the girls as much as I did. But first the El Paso County Sheriff Deputy had to escort my mother, and I over to Patric's grandmother house to get our daughter. It scared her to see all of this at such a young age. He was permitted visitation rights on the weekend, but was ordered to stay from my apartment.

Chapter Three

Out of nowhere my mother saying screaming " in the blood of jesus!"That's the only thing that made my dad stop beating him down.It was crazy scene I must say. But my dad told me to get my things and get in the car with our daughter.I did my things, and get in the car with our daughter. I did but you guys know how it is when you're in love with someone. I'm the typing of woman who believe in his good side, which is not a good example for my daughters, and sons at the time . I had to learn to love myself in order to be able to love someone else." Never let anyone abuse you , or use you, and do not feel guilty about your situation." You know when you're in love because there is nothing you won't do for that person. They stay on your mind. You don't want to make a mistake. You only want to make them happy. Sometimes you might not eat, or sleep over them. You always want to be on your best.There is an odd soul connection between the two of you.You defend them against all odds. When their hurting, it hurts you as well. As I took my vows, just like many others, I wanted to believe in what me in Patrick had. We were the greatest front marriage known to mankind. I remember the time I tasted my own blood. Patric, and I were talking smack to one another, and trust me it got heated. At one point in time in our marriage all we did was fight. He said something to me , and I shot some quick remark back at him. You know the kind of remark that gets under your skin that's what I hit him with. Well I guess he could not take , and punched me dead in my face. Right to the lips his fist went. Big mistake. I fought him back like Tina Turner. He hit me again , and pushed me hard as he could. I fell to the ground the impact. I had to put a protection order against Patric for the following reasons? I was twenty two years old at the time. Patric climbed through my apartment window, which at the time was a bottom floor apartment at 907 East Santa Fe street. Most people call it by its formal name- Payne Chapel Housing over there by Hillside. But anyway, Patrick took the screen off my daughter's window, and had my daughter Imani in his arms already when I came to check on her. I was like what the hell !He was calling for our other daughter lovely to jump in his arms as well. I ran out of the building as fast as I could, but Patrick took off running like a track star with our daughter in his arms. By the time I reached the parking lot, the car speeded away with Patric, and my daughter gone. m y heart broke into a million pieces at that moment. He had planned the whole thing quite querulously if you ask me, but that stuff work. He had been stalking the apartment for a few weeks to pull off a move like that. I got calls from him, threatening to not bring our daughter back to me. Saying things like he was going to keep her away from me forever. My dad told me not to call the police on Patric , because he said Imani was his daughter as well , and no harm would come to her in his care. After a week of all that nonsense I called the Police, and was told I had to put a protection order against him. I mean we were Husband , and wife, so he had rights to the rights to the girls as much as I did. But first the El Paso County Sheriff Deputy had to escort my mother, and I over to Patric's grandmother house to get our daughter. It scared her to see all of this at such a young age. He was permitted visitation rights on the weekend, but was ordered to stay from my apartment.

Chapter Four (Deal with Your Drama or Not!)

At this time of my life it became quite clear that I was a dream magnet. Meaning whatever I did, drama seemed to follow me. I didn't want it to be like that , but it was.Patrick found himself playing tennis with El Paso County Jail (CJC),and the Community Corrections Comcor. Apparently he had driving charges , and domestic violent charges that he had spaced out. I started hanging out with my neighbor who goes by the name , Johnnie Mae. I also worked at Ihop that year, filing for my taxes which gave me back $ 3,000 dollars.I brought my first car with that money.Unaware Patric was already robbing banks by now, which was a true shock to me, seeing how I thought he was only selling drugs.He robbed banks in the Colorado Springs ares for five years before getting caught, and landing his butt in a federal camp. His crime partner got life in prison. While Patric only did fifthteen months , if it adds up. Anyway, one night hanging with Johnny Mae I seen this guy by the name of Pony tail, and we gave each other a hug. The music blaring as we played pool for an hour, and a couple shots of Hennessy later. I know it was wrong , seeing I was technically a married woman, and my husband was in jail, but hey guilty don't talk much. If it makes it any better we already liked each other from way back in the day. This relationship became a long term affair very fast. Patric started hearing rumors, but he didn't need to hear rumors, but he didn't need to hear rumors he was still watching me. Donnelly chess, which was supposed to be Ponytails best friend told Patric what we were doing. (messing around). As crazy as it sounds but Patrick was really trying to have something special with me, but it was too late. I was gone off the coldest drug known to mankind …. Guilty revenge. That same year I got approved for a twenty thousand dollar loan from the bank to start my own business. Strangely to know Patric and I were still together in one odd way. We both lied to the whole world about who lovely's father was …Ponytail . I finished beauty school , and took my state my state boards test during all this madness. Instead of opening up my own beauty salon, I Got talked into investing my money into a soul food restaurant called (This Is It.) The restaurant was right next door to a club called the Prime Time", which was up, and jumping, oddly the owner of the club found himself in search of a business friend, and I was too eager to get in ,on the action. Come to find out the owner of a sucker , which he found me . Patris was the biggest lollipop though. At that time , I felt so bad for cheating on him, that I just right along with what was going down.

The owner who went by name of black at the time was smoking crack in his blunts. Plus he was on other drugs as well, which I found out later, on. Patric looked up to him for his jazzy word play, and fancy way dressing. So yeah it's true , black , and his daughters ran so much game on Patric ,because he was young, dumb, and full of cum. Not to add Patric was a square to the street life. Now picture me sitting back watching these city slickers run grade A , who despite my warings, found it in his intention to invest my money in this restaurant. (not amart).i won't lie I wanted to invest this business proposition to be real as he did ,but my wine glass only drinks the finest taste. Meaning you have to wake up pretty damn early to get jump on me. This was how it added up on paper if you care to know.I would work the day time , with Patric for the breakfast , and lunch specials , and black his daughters would work the night dinner specials, All the money in the register draws was supposed to to come to me. I'm sure ,I don't have to tell you they did not, and within six months we had nothing. We'll I had something ,but Patrick had nothing but a new crack habit, and disappointed wife, What do you do, when your entire marriage is a sham? Deal with your drama, or not.

Chapter Five " Moving Too Fast"

At the age of twenty five years old I was going to Everest College for their paralegal program, and working for school #11. I also ran an escort service that mainly surrounded couples, and swingers. My baby brother (Shugg) did not know this at the time, seeing how he got out of prison two weeks after I was stabbed in the head, neck, stomach, thigh, and hand. The man I was seeing at that time acted like he was down to be a part of that life, but he was not ready to take it to that level. Even though Patric, and I were legally still married nothing stopped me from doing what I wanted to do. I was being a very bad girl. I met this guy named Ant, who gave me the desire I was chasing at the time. He paid me $900 dollars one time to turn his wife out.It seems he had wanted her to be a little more exotic like in the bedroom department. Her name was Angela, she was very beautiful, but unaware how to use her energy to control the room, as well ,as her marriage. I schooled her to everything she needed to know, but I felt bad because I was sleeping with her husband. (The nerve of me, I know). I danced with her in this club, and made her feel like the most beautiful woman in the world. She was like a pill you had to open up to fully enjoy guys out there who think your lady, or mate is satisfied. You never quite know what she is thinking about your dried up four polay. Trust me when I tell you to step up your game. Think of your mate as your favorite piece of pie, you never can get enough of showing them true admiration. You know how they say every young lady must come into her own when woman hood knocks on her door. Let's just say I was ready to answer that door bell when it was my time. Twenty seven old, with crazy sense of direction would be the best way describe me at that point of time. My baby brother (Shugg) finally made it out of prison, and came to live with me. He was so tall he couldn't even walk in the door without ducking his head. The first thing we did was joined (K.G.) at the studio. Knowing what I know now . I would not have took him over to such a foul place with such a heartless person. Anyway Shugg is my baby brother, but his also a very handsome young man. So when I tell you all the females were glued to him, it is only half of what I mean. His 6'4 , 250 lbs with waves all over his head. Perfect teeth , and a very smooth voice. (He's a young Billy Dee Williams) Don't tell him I said that because seeing it would go right to his big head. It wasn't long before Everett helped me move out of my current apartment, and into a better place for us to kick it. He brought his little fan club with him as well . Some were cool, ans some were about to get choked out by me. One of the females who enjoyed his company donated a living room set to me. He also had a Native American chick named Heather who I did not like at all. I expressed how I felt for her a numerous of times . She just wasn't my cup of coffee in people. The first day I met her, I thought she was going to overdose on cocaine, and she beat up her little sister. It wasn't long before Shugg found out my lifestyle , and tried to take over my business. I remember being at the club one night , and this female said " after party at your house right !" I was like hell no it aint! Boy was I wrong. I came home to see my brother , with two females getting it in with all their faces white as snow. They were sniffing cocaine for everybody who doesn't speak the lingo. You could imagine my state of shock seeing my brother going in without a care in the world. I was kind of happy for him, seeing how I knew he had just got out of prison, and wanted to live it up, but I was pissed as well. I don't like alot of people in my business. Kendall had sex with them our whole crew would drink for free the whole night. I thought he had brought the bar out, but come to find out he had pimped Kendall out. I remember hearing him shout " everybody get whatever you want!" I myself had five shots of something that cost twenty dollars a shot. The atmosphere was very live, and I was told my brother to tell Heather , and Kendall to stop passing his gun around. They were playing with it like two little kids excited about the thought of danger. He always said that the clip of the gun was broke, and he did not want them to get shot , or shoot themselves. Soon after that Shugg , and Kendall started dancing on the floor, and I could see Heather did not like that. Meanwhile a white lady asked me if my breast were fake? I laughed at first , and calmly stated they were real. She paid me to feel them, I was like why not? She did. All it took was one night for my whole life to change. My baby brother came over my house like he always did with the chick heather. His side piece, and he were already getting lite off cocaine. I remember he had fifth thousand dollars in his pockets, and he was with three of his homies. He told me to go pick up kendallk from mother's house, who was another one of his girls. So I had Heather take me over there to get her, and we all met back up at the bar which across the street from the Newport Square Apartments. We were preparing to have a good night out on the town, unaware that the feds were watching us the whole time. There's some things I can't talk about so please forgive if I don't too much into detail. I will say that women get jealous when their not the main attraction. My brother had kendall have sex with six men in the bathroom of the bar. Three of them were his home boys that came with him, and the other guy was the bartender. Than there was the owner of the club, and last but not least the manager of the club. Shugg made a deal with the bartender , and the manager that if.

Chapter Six: Could it be love

Soon after that Shugg , and Kendall started dancing on the floor, and I could see Heather did not like that. Meanwhile a white lady asked me if my breast were fake? I laughed at first , and calmly stated they were real. She paid me to feel them, I was like why not? She did. All it took was one night for my whole life to change. My baby brother came over my house like he always did with the chick heather. His side piece, and he were already getting lite off cocaine. I remember he had fifth thousand dollars in his pockets, and he was with three of his homies. He told me to go pick up kendallk from mother's house, who was another one of his girls. So I had Heather take me over there to get her, and we all met back up at the bar which across the street from the Newport Square Apartments. We were preparing to have a good night out on the town, unaware that the feds were watching us the whole time. There's some things I can't talk about so please forgive if I don't too much into detail. I will say that women get jealous when their not the main attraction. My brother had kendall have sex with six men in the bathroom of the bar. Three of them were his home boys that came with him, and the other guy was the bartender. Than there was the owner of the club, and last but not least the manager of the club. Shugg made a deal with the bartender , and the manager that if.

Chapter. Seven Dead End Road"

A few drinks later my head started to spin like a merry go round. So I remember telling my brother I was about to leave. He told me to take Kendalkl with me, and we would meet back up at my house later. Once we got out to the parking lot, who, who knew our lives would be changed forever. The parking lot was packed with people trying to get in , and out the club. A real congested scene. Soon as we got in Heather's car all I remember is Heather trying to run my brother over. She was going thirty miles per hour, and a hail of bullets hit the car. The inside , and outside of Heather's car was tattooed with bullets holes. I could hardly breathe from the rush of thoughts running through my head. That's when I heard kendall say "I've been shot !" I opened the door to the car to let her out. She was shot in the head , and probably in a state of shock to even , know it. I must say she is definitely a strong female because she had enough power to run across the street to the apartments called the Greentree Apartments. My brother ran with us to the Apartments to hide from all the commotion that was going down. I Remember we all sat, and watched Heather ,from the Greentree Apartments window, as she called 911. The police , and firefighters helped her get in the back of the ambulance. Kendall was with my brother (Shugg) , and yes she was still shot. I gave her a t-shirt of cocaine to sniff, hoping that would take her pain away. She later told me she didn't even feel anything. (I was like I bet you didn't Tony " Freskin"Montana). I walked across the street to the Newport Apartments, and went home. I called my other brother Tony, and him to go pick up Shugg , and Kendall. They all got caught up by the police. My brother is serving a forty year sentence for that night as this book is being made. It truly hurts my heart to know how things turned out. "People believe their eyes, and lie to their souls . See I am different A rare breed indeed, someone who understand life , and all things people need. See I know what it feels like to be betrayed , but I have held the knife as well, someone who can tell you about the perfect balance, and everything that dwells.See I have been in love before . I have hated even more, Someone who can smile at pain, and still cry on the floor. See I know what comes from faithfulness, I have walked in shoes of the lost souls, someone who the world has forsaken, left there bloody , and cold. See I do not look at life for What it is, but what it could be . Do you know what I see? At the age of twenty eight ,I looked forward to my life as seeing it for , what it was … a mom. With all that had happened I seen life through a new pair eyes. I understood I had to move on with my life, and raise my kids. But don't get it misunderstood when I say, I had to start being a mother, because I was always focused on my kids. I just had to put a closer view on the glasses, I was looking through. I was hopeful about moving on with life, but I was young at heart like many people who make mistakes in life . Plus I was focused on getting my baby brother a paid lawyer. "See your life through the right pair of glasses".

Chapter: Eight " Hope Finds A Home"

I gave birth to a beautiful little boy who I named after my baby brother Shugg. I promised him ,I would do that for him . With high hopes Lil Shugg. I promised him I would go through life, and fulfill all the things my brother was supposed to do. As you know my brothers , and I were not raised in the streets like most of the books you read about doing the wrong things, and making them right. My parents always wanted the right things for their children like many parents do. Back to my crazy life,Shugg's dad moved back to St. Louis, MO when he was eight months old. His name was James.

James had to fight for custody of his daughter, back in St. Louis since his daughter's mother was on heroin.James , and I were more like friends, and we both knew long distance relationships don't always work out.I'll give him credit he wanted us to move back St. Louis with him, but James stayed in the projects. I'm My father worked all his life to make sure none of his kids lived below their means, and I wanted to honor his hard work, by making sure

I did the same thing. For the next few years, I worked at Wilson, and never went out on the town. I was super mom day in, and day out. My kids are so spoiled til this day, because they know mommy loves them dearly. When I turned thirty years old, I went to this club called the "Old School ', and that was also the first time .I had committed to drinking since the night my brother got locked up. I had a good time that night, and took my happy self home to my kids. At the age thirty one, I got pregnant with my daughter " Essence" who is my flower child. She looks at you like she can see you whole life in her eyes. Her dad went to prison, when I was four months pregnant with her. When Essence turned six months old he got out, and I was the only family he had. As I recall on August 16,2014 I received a six thousand dollar settlement from Dollar Tree. It was for my daughter''s slip , and fall injury. I moved back to the Fireside Apartments, and brought , new furniture & a new car. Things were very nice for three months. I felt so at one with myself.

When the Odds Are Against You
The time is now!
The Fight of your life.

A time to be one with who we strive to be. A time to

understand why?

Why do we explore ?

Why do we ask?

I believe we long to discover ourselves.

To see what we are truly made of . A time to dig deep .

A time to give up the thing that holds us back , and a time to keep.

Chapter Nine " Just When You Think You Have Seen It All"

2014 around Thanksgiving Essence's father released from prison, but I did not know he had a drug problem. He was smoking Meth like a train coming down the railroad. I was knocked up with my other son Deaundrae who is Essence's brother. Young people here is something to always remember people will be themselves no matter how you treat them. One day I looked up to see the father of my two youngest kids on Crime Stoppers. The police were looking for him. Now this part will make you guys laugh. I use to have this friend who went by the name gay Mike. We were very close until he told me he sucked my baby father's penis for meth one day. I was like "hell nah!" I also found out later that the father of my kids was riding around town with transgender side piece smoking meth. Just when you think you have seen it all, something like that pops up to throw you for loop. I wasn't mad , or anything like that , I thought it was funny. (Keep it on the down low.) My heart been through alot thus far in my life, and trust me when I say all the times were not as bad as they seem. I've always been a fighter at heart. I didn't let people run over me, or treat any kind of way. This is something I passed down to all my kids, trying to give them the power of the mind , and heart. June 2, 2015 I gave birth to my son, Deaundrae, we who we all call baby bro. All of my kids were in the delivery room, some had their little eyes closed, but they understood their baby brother was coming into the world. My dad showed up late ,but he was there with a smile on his face. He said " you women are crazy to be having kids," because he hates to see me go through pain. Soon after that I started working at the Olympic Training Center in Colorado Springs, CO as a prep cook every weekend. I also worked in Cripple Creek (at the gaming casino) which was pretty fun. In July my daughter Imani , and I started our gift card business. We had gift cards for every thing you could think of. King Soopers, Walmart, and Sam's Club. We had them all. I never paid cash for gas I remember.

What We Bring Back

Wth the type of money I made off the gift cards, I was able to not only afford to throw the best baby shower known to mankind, but I had the best that life offered me. As stated before my poor Little kids are addicted to the finer things because of me. They wear Jordans for fun. Their clothes are top of the line when they go to school, or out with their friends. It wasn't long before ,I found myself back with Ponytail as if that was a good choice. I started off by contacting him, because my other baby's father stole some meth from me. I needed some muscle to be around if things got out of hand. Plus I didn't want to get my hands dirty, so I let Ponytail do most of the pushing of the drugs. I gave him two ounces of meth to sell, but

I should told him to keep it , and get away from me, seeing how the next chain of events changed how I viewed the world.

If Only….

Chapter Ten " Thank You God… for real !"

If only it was true that all woman who suffer from domestic violent cases were completely innocent. Yeah right ! Or should I just speak for myself.

Because I started my fight with Ponytail.

I hit him first, as most of us women do when something gets the better of our emotions.

I hit about ten good times before he even reacted to my assault on him.

He tried to swing back but was too slow, than he cornered me in the alley way, of his house.

The fight lead out to his back yard that did not face anything that no one could see.

Once he had me cornered he grabbed my neck, and hair in one tight hand of his.

I felt like my neck was broke.

He threw me on the ground in swift like motion.

Slim Chances

I swear the devil was using me because I said , when I get up I gonna kick your ass ! "

Plus I was disrespecting his manhood , and his neighborhood as he held me down.

That must have struck a nerve, because he kicked me repeatedly. As I laid there completely out of breath .I thought that was the end of our little fight, but I was wrong. I felt his hand grab the back of my neck, and pull me up like a rag doll.

Than he snatched my pants down, and started having his way with me from behind.

I hated it.

In a rage he picked me up , and threw me in the trash can as my head hit the bottom. I still told myself I'm about to get his ass.

I was hurt over , and over again, he didn't know who he was messing with. My body was hurt very bad as I climbed out of the trash can the devil was talking in my ear.

Saying " you have to kill him".

I was like "o.k. How do I do this ? "

Than I saw my kids flash in my head a few times as I walked up to his back door which was locked. I couldn't let him get away with this act of war.

I was so mad ,I wanted to do something to his mother, and sister as well.

He needs to pay that's all I could think about. I didn't want him to think, I was like other girls who cried, and walked away with a broke heart.

My dad , and my be brothers raised a tough young lady, and I would show him.

L kicked his back door as hard as , I could. It didn't move at first, but I got it open after three more kicks. Once in the house he told me to seriously to sit my ass down before he really got pissed off. He said he wanted to talk.

I was like talk !

Fool I'm about to try to take your head off with one swing. He was smoking a blunt as he spoke " look I don't want to fight with you anymore. Breath, but that didn't stop me from plotting in my head as he spoke.

I wanted to do many things to him that I started blinking very fast. I picked up the Hennessy bottle very slow, and drunk from it.

He told me to be a lady , and get some glasses. I watched him light up another blunt, as passed it to me , after taking a few puffs off of it.

I inhaled it as my lungs felt this funny feeling.

I got even more mad when he started smiling like he just got away with murder.

He said " you going to pay to get my door fixed !"

L asked him if he was smoking my product?

Than I repeated myself.

" Have you been smoking my stuff with these ghostly stupid hoes !"

I started yelling at him in a crazy tone. Next thing I know I kicked him out of the chair he was sitting in.

The fight was back on (second round) as I caught my breath.

That's all I was waiting for. He fell to the floor, as L jumped on him like a wild animal. Picture his head between my legs, and beating his face like a teddy bear, that you're mad at. I was talking smack as I hit him as hard as I could. " Who you think I am ?"

"You thought I would let you get away that bull shit ! "

" He played dead like a possum, and I climbed off of him.

(Not so fast.)

He tripped me.

I thought he was going to get his off the table so I crawled toward the doggy door.

He caught my feet, and dragged me back to the kitchen floor.

I got lost somehow with all intentions to run out of the front door, but something told me to look out the window.

It was the police.

I told Pony tail the police were outside.

But he still wanted to get the better of me.

They saw us through the window, and knocked on the door.

How could we explain my bloody pants, and torn ears…

That looked crazy swollen by now.

Not to add I was in my bra with no shoes on in the winter time.

He told them h9is ear drum was busted, and he could not hear them, trying to play stupid.

They arrested both our asses.

When I arrived at the police station , I started feeling all the drugs in my system.

I had sixteen charges that got dropped, but I got a 2nd degree assault on a nurse . I pimp slapped her.

The county jail doesn't have any video of this incident, but since the nurse was injured. I took a plea deal for my actions.

I got closed out for six months for my actions in the county.

So my prison time started off kind of rough.

I made the best of it, but I couldn't fake being away from my kids hurt my heart to the core.

As I looked around in the cold cell, I started asking myself, where did I go wrong?

Chapter Eleven " The Future Has A Face of Beauty"

The best way I would describe prison is like a chess board, and guess who are the ponds?
I swear there are so many fake people in prison, I'm surprised that mannequins still have jobs on the streets. They have the bible crew in prison, who walk around like they are super holy. But every time you see them they are talking behind others backs. (kind of like real churches on the outside) than you have the wannabe thug girls who try their hardest to convince people they are boys. But the truth is they usually have little lick buddies who will do anything for a cup of noodles. (I mean anything !) Then don't get me started on the C.O.'s that come through the door like they have never seen a female on the outsides.
 (Thirsty alert)
I have a very opinionated personality, so prison presented a huge challenge for me.
But I made it you guys. I made it.

You ask me why you should stay in school, and out of the streets?
Well when I got to prison they had a herpes, and hepatitis outbreak. Have you ever seen herpes in someone's eye ?
Trust me you'll never eat meatballs in spaghetti anymore.
They have females who suck females private area for strawberry cakes!
That is so true.
They trade coffee for sex.
Young people of the world you do not want to be headed to prison, with your mother crying a fistful of tears.
Be smarter than me please I beg you.
You don't have to be a gangsta to get caught up in prison anymore. They have people from all walks of life in their.
Rich kids, poor kids, smart kids, and most of all confused kids.

As I leave you with these wise words from a great person, I ask that you take them for what they mean to you.
" You can run with the wind , or up against it… but the wind could care less if you blew away tomorrow"
(check out the three poems by my favorite poet on the next pages.)

Thank you guys for supporting me, and listening to my strong story.

Love Yall ....Marquita

Gorging on the dead

The one you neglected

The one you chose

The one you selected

Again and agian- they just pecked it

Broke the mirror within

No matter what it reflected?

Ripping flesh from bone

Soul from body

I yelled out " help !" " Please help me somebody !"

No one came

So as you know they ate , and they ate

Until I was no more

Leaving a bloody spot, left there to rot, on the world's floor.

Within a divided soul

Who do you trust ?

Beauty

I watch them from afar .

Souls trapped in a jar, with aspirations of tar.

They go to war with their own hearts.

Tiny scars too small to care about, Isolated stars of a broken constellation.

Staring out the window in a period of doubt.

Can't scream… can't see… can't shout …. Can't find their way out.

Fighting battles never won before the first gun is fired.

Let there, on the battlefield of life, wounded, and tired

Afraid to stand up.

Too strong to fall down

Watching the future become the past

A ghostly merry- go -round

Telling themselves to be stern

But then again the time of life are grime

I judge their reflection on the mirror

Sadly to say I'm just like them,

Trapped behind red glass

You want to know a

Friends are rare

You know them by their actions

Their will to truly care

Their will to be there… right beside you (in your ear)

Telling you things for own good

Showing you

Helping you

As they should

Not getting you deeper in trouble

Not saying " Come on man we won't get caught !"

Than soon as you do (like always)

They are the first to say (it was not my fault)

Friends understand your value

Friends love to see your true worth

Friends smile when you smile, and do not drag your name through the dirt.

Friends are rare, they help you prevail, and here is a little truth

There is not that many in jail… and less in prison.

You Find Out Who your Friends Are.

"Pick your friends don't let your friends pick you"

When you pick your friends yourself, it allows you to not

Only see the quality of your friend picking abilities, but it also

grants you the power of

Seeing value in others.

Like I tell all my kids, and many others who have the pleasure,of

meeting me, strive for greatest. Now I know you feel compelled

after reading my book to ask the question of the hour. What have I

strived for up until this point?

I answer that question with a statement I still live by as, I strive for

happiness.

What does that mean you ask ?

Happiness is something you can't buy in an store.

You can't steal it, or hide it under a rock somewhere.

It has to take place in your life at a time when you need it the

most.

Happiness could rest in a child's smile, but you are thinking about

your lazy coworker who always borrows money from you at lunch

time.

Happiness could be in a beautiful song, but you can't hear it because the loud noise in your crazy head.

Happiness is all around us every day , but we must be willing to get out of our own way to cherish it's beauty.

It's your turn.

I'm out.

Beauty

www.ingramcontent.com/pod-product-compliance
Lightning Source LLC
Chambersburg PA
CBHW052207110526
44591CB00012B/2108